Science 1

Third Edition

bju press®

Greenville, South Carolina

Note:
The fact that materials produced by other publishers may be referred to in this volume does not constitute an endorsement of the content or theological position of materials produced by such publishers. Any references and ancillary materials are listed as an aid to the student or the teacher and in an attempt to maintain the accepted academic standards of the publishing industry.

SCIENCE 1
THIRD EDITION

Coordinating Author
Joyce Garland

Author
Janet E. Snow

Project Editor
Naomi Viola

Page Layout
Linda Hastie

Designer
Michael Asire

Project Managers
Faith Larson
Roxana P. Pérez

Consultants
Bill Harmon
Ann Larson
Robin Scroggins
Sherri Vick

Bible Integration
Brian Collins
Bryan Smith

Cover Design
Elly Kalagayan

Front Cover Illustration
Aaron Dickey

Back Cover Illustration
Matt Bjerk

Photo Acquisition
Rita Mitchell
LaDonna Ryggs

Illustrators
Courtney Godbey
Lynda Slattery

Photograph credits appear on pages 159–60.

© 2011, 2017 BJU Press
Greenville, South Carolina 29614
First Edition © 1975 BJU Press. Second Edition © 1989, 1998, 2003 BJU Press

ISBN 978-1-62856-295-8

15 14 13 12 11 10 9 8 7 6 5 4 3 2 1

Welcome to *Science 1*

Take a trip through this book. See amazing things in God's world. You can use science to learn about the world. You can use science to show love. God gave us the job of caring for His world. You will learn how to use God's world wisely. You can use what you learn to praise God for His care for you.

FIND OUT about God's world using your five senses. Learn how the water on the earth moves the same way over and over. Study about tame and wild animals. Find out how sound moves. Understand which parts of plants you eat.

EXPERIENCE how your sense of smell affects your sense of taste. Observe and record the weather as a weatherman. Discover whether washing your hands helps get rid of germs. Make an instrument and play a song. Complete an experiment to learn why it is hard to see the stars during the day. Remember to praise and thank our Creator as you travel through this book.

Enjoy the fun trip!

Contents

Senses 1

Your Senses

God made the world.
God made you too.
God wants you to find out about the
world He made.
He gave you ways to find out about
the world.
God gave you five **senses**.

Your five senses are sight, touch, smell, taste, and hearing.
You can use your senses to find out about God's world.
What you find out about the world is called **science**.

What do you use to learn about God's world?

Seeing

Sight is one of your senses.
You see with your eyes.

You can see the sizes of things.

You can see the shapes of things.

You can see the colors of things.

You see many different things.
Your sense of sight helps you find
out about God's world.

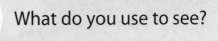 What do you use to see?

5

Touching

Touch is one of your senses.
You use your hands and fingers to touch.

You touch hard and
soft things.

You touch hot and cold things.

You touch bumpy and smooth things.

You touch many different things.
Your sense of touch helps you find out
about God's world.

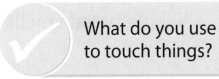
What do you use
to touch things?

Smelling

Smell is one of your senses.
You use your nose to smell.

You smell things that smell good.
Flowers smell good.
Baking bread smells good.

You also smell things
that smell bad.
A skunk smells bad.
Dirty socks smell bad.

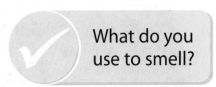

You smell many different things.
Your sense of smell helps you find
out about God's world.

✓ What do you
use to smell?

9

Tasting

Taste is one of your senses.
You use your tongue and
mouth to taste.

You taste things that
are sweet.
You taste things that
are sour.

You taste things that are salty.
You taste things that are bitter.

You taste many different things.
Your sense of taste helps you
find out about God's world.

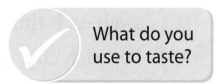

What do you
use to taste?

Smell and Taste

Smell and taste are not the same. They are two different senses. But can you taste something without smelling it? Find out how what you smell affects what you taste.

Purpose

Find out how your sense of smell affects your sense of taste.

Materials
prepared cups
8 cotton swabs
Activity Manual

Procedure

1. Pinch your nose shut. Use a cotton swab to taste what is in cup A.
2. In your Activity Manual, record what flavor you tasted.
3. Pinch your nose shut and taste what is in each of the other cups. Use a new cotton swab each time.
4. For each cup, record what you taste.

5. Taste what is in each cup again. Do not pinch your nose shut this time.

6. Record what each flavor tasted like when you could also smell it.

Conclusions

▶ Did things taste the same when you could not smell them?

▶ Does your sense of smell affect your sense of taste?

Hearing

Hearing is one of your senses.
You use your ears to hear.

You hear loud and soft sounds.

You hear bangs and whistles.

You hear birds singing.
You hear people talking.

You hear many different things.
Hearing is a way to find out
about God's world.

God gave you many ways to find
out about His world.
You can use your senses.
You can be a **scientist**.
Scientists learn about God's world.
They use their senses.

✓ What do you use to hear?

The Weather

The Weather

It is hot.

It is windy.

It is snowing.

These are ways we talk about the weather.

The **weather** is what the air outside is like.

The weather changes from day to day.
One day may be sunny and clear.
The next day may be cloudy and rainy.
A **weatherman** tells us about the weather.

What does a weatherman do?

Temperature

The **temperature** is how hot or cold it is.
A weatherman tells about the temperature
of the air.
He tells whether it is hot or cold.

A weatherman uses a **thermometer** to find
out the temperature.
The thermometer has numbers on it.
The weatherman uses the numbers to
tell us the temperature of the air.

The temperature changes during the day.
In the daytime the sun warms the air.
The temperature goes up.

At nighttime the sun does not warm the air.
The temperature goes down.

✓ What does a weatherman use to find out the temperature?

Wind

A weatherman tells about the wind.
Wind is moving air.

Warm air rises.
Cool air sinks.
The changes in air cause wind.

Wind moves things.
It moves leaves on trees.
It moves sailboats.

The wind also moves flags.
You can use a flag to tell how hard the wind is blowing.

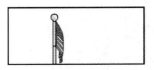 You may say the wind is calm.
The wind is not blowing much.

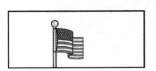 You may say there is a light wind.
The wind is blowing a little bit.

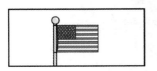 You may say the wind is strong.
The wind is blowing a lot.

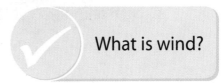 What is wind?

Clouds

The water on the earth moves the same way over and over.
This is called a **cycle**.

Water comes out of the air.

Water goes up into the air.

Water falls to the ground.

The water in the air causes clouds.
Clouds are made of tiny drops of water in the sky.

A weatherman tells us about the clouds.

 He may say it is clear.
There are no clouds.

 He may say it is partly cloudy.
There are some clouds.

 He may say it is cloudy.
There are many clouds.

✔ What causes clouds?

Water from the Sky

Clouds have many drops of water.
The drops may join together.
This makes the drops get heavy.
Then they fall to the ground.

A weatherman tells us about water
that falls to the ground.

He may say it is raining.

He may say it is sleeting.

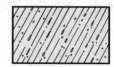

He may say it is hailing.

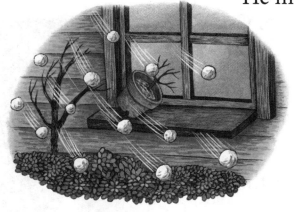

He may say it is snowing.

 What are four kinds of water that fall to the ground?

The Weatherman

The weather is part of God's world.

A weatherman uses his senses to find out about the air outside.

He **observes** the weather.

He uses tools as he observes the weather.

A weatherman writes down what he finds out.

He makes maps and charts.

He **records** what he finds out about the weather.

A weatherman tells others what he finds out.
He **reports** the weather.
He tells about God's world.

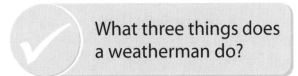
What three things does a weatherman do?

Weather Watching

A weatherman observes the weather. He records what he observes. You can also be a weatherman. In this activity you will observe and record the weather for five days.

Purpose

Observe and record the weather.

Procedure

Materials
thermometer
small flag
prepared symbols
Activity Manual

1. Take the thermometer and small flag outside.
2. Read the thermometer.
3. Hold up the flag. Observe the flag to see how hard the wind is blowing.
4. Observe the clouds.
5. Observe whether any rain, sleet, hail, or snow is falling.

6. Discuss what you observed. Fill in the first day on the chart in your Activity Manual.

7. Observe the weather for four more days. Make sure to record what you observe each day.

Conclusion

▶ What things about the weather changed during the week?

Seasons

The Seasons

Spring, summer, autumn, and winter
are times of the year.
They are called seasons.
A **season** is a time of year.
Each year has these four seasons.

God made the seasons.
They are part of His world.
We find out about His world when we
study the seasons He made.

spring

summer

The seasons change.
Spring changes to summer.
Summer changes to autumn.
Autumn changes to winter.
Winter changes to spring again.
The seasons are a cycle.

✓ What is a season?

autumn

winter

Spring

Spring begins in March.
In spring the daytime gets longer.
We get more sunlight than we do in winter.
The temperature gets warm.
Spring rains come.

Spring is a time of planting.
Some people plant seeds.
Seeds sprout and start to grow.
Trees get new leaves.
Flowers grow.

In spring baby animals
are born.
Birds build nests and
lay eggs.

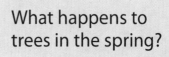

What happens to
trees in the spring?

Summer

Summer comes after spring.
Summer begins in June.
The daytime is long in summer.
We get more sunlight than we do
in other seasons.
The temperature gets hot.

Summer is a time for growing.
Plants grow bigger in summer.
Some trees and bushes grow fruit.
Vegetables grow and get ripe.

Baby animals eat and grow.
Baby birds begin to fly and
leave their nests.

In the summer, is the
daytime long or short?

Autumn

Autumn comes after summer.
Autumn begins in September.
The daytime starts to get shorter than
in summer.
We get less sunlight than in summer.
It gets dark earlier.
The temperature gets cool.

Leaves on some trees change colors.
They fall to the ground.

Autumn is a time of harvest.
Plants stop growing.
Fruits and vegetables are picked.

Some animals gather food for winter.
Other animals move to a new place.
They go to a place that will have more
food in winter.
In spring the animals will come back.

✓ What happens to some
leaves in autumn?

Winter

Winter comes after autumn.
Winter begins in December.
The daytime is short.
We get less sunlight than we do
in other seasons.
The temperature gets cold.
Sometimes snow falls.

Winter is a time of resting.
Many trees have no leaves.
Some plants die.
Other plants rest.
They will start to grow again in spring.

Some animals sleep
through winter.
They will wake up again
in spring.

When winter is over,
spring comes.
The cycle of the seasons
begins again.

The seasons change, but God does not.
He cares for His world all the time.
He gives each thing what it needs in
every season.

✔ In what season do plants
and animals rest?

ACTIVITY

Seasons Book

We learn about God's world by using our senses. As a scientist you record what you learn. This activity will let you show what your senses help you learn about the seasons.

Purpose

Show what you learn about each season by using your senses.

Materials
prepared pages
pictures
glue
scissors
Activity Manual

Procedure

1. Each person in your group should choose a different season.

2. Get pages from your teacher.

3. Think about what you see in your season. Cut out pictures showing things you see. Glue the pictures on the page labeled *Sight*. You may also draw pictures.

4. Do the same for each of your other senses.

5. Follow your teacher's directions to complete the poem in your Activity Manual.

6. Follow your teacher's directions to put your group's book together. Start your book with spring.

Conclusion

▶ Can you use each of your senses to find out about each season?

Health and Safety

Your Body

God made you.

He made you just the way He wanted you to be.

Maybe you are tall.

Maybe you have freckles.

Maybe you need to wear glasses.

God made each part of you.

God made people to be different.
Each person is special to God.

God made your body.
He gave you the job of caring for it.

There are ways to take care of your body.
You should eat food that is good for you.
You should run and play outside.
You should get the rest you need.
Doing these things helps you be healthy.
A **healthy** person is not sick or hurt.

✓ What are three ways to take care of your body?

Healthy Habits

Habits are things you do over and over again.
Healthy habits help you care for your body.

You take baths to keep clean.
You wash and comb your hair.
You brush your teeth.
These are healthy habits.

Some habits help keep germs away.
Germs are things that can make you sick.
You cannot see germs, but you can help
get rid of them.
Wash your hands with soap and water.
Keep cuts in your skin clean.

Some habits help keep germs
away from other people.
Cover your mouth when you
cough.
Use a tissue when you sneeze.
Doing these things will help
other people not get sick.

Why should you cover your
mouth when you cough?

ACTIVITY

Clean Hands

Are your hands clean? You are often told to wash your hands. Washing helps get rid of some germs. In this activity you will see that hands that look clean can still have germs.

Problem

Does washing hands help get rid of germs?

Materials
2 gelatin cups
2 labeled bags
cotton swabs
shoebox
Activity Manual

Procedure

1. Take the gelatin cup out of the bag labeled *Dirty*. Follow your teacher's directions about touching things.

2. Rub a cotton swab on your hands. Gently make zigzag lines on the gelatin with the swab. Then put the cup back in the bag and seal it.

3. Wash your hands carefully and dry them. Try not to touch anything.

4. Rub a clean cotton swab on your hands. Take the gelatin cup out of the bag labeled *Clean*. Gently make lines on top of the gelatin. Put the cup back in the bag and seal it.

5. Put the bags in the shoebox. Put the box in a warm place.

6. Observe the gelatin daily. Record what you see in your Activity Manual.

Conclusions

▶ Which gelatin cup had the most germs? How do you know?

▶ Did washing get rid of all the germs?

Your Teeth

You use your **teeth** to cut and chew food.
God made your teeth strong.

God gave you two sets of teeth.
Your first set of teeth came in when you were
a baby.
As you grow, your baby teeth fall out.
A new tooth grows in place of your baby tooth.
The new tooth is bigger.
It will not fall out.

You need to take care of your teeth.
Use a toothbrush and toothpaste to
brush your teeth.
Floss once a day.
Doing these things helps your
teeth stay healthy.

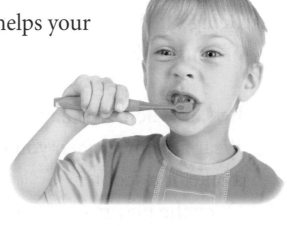

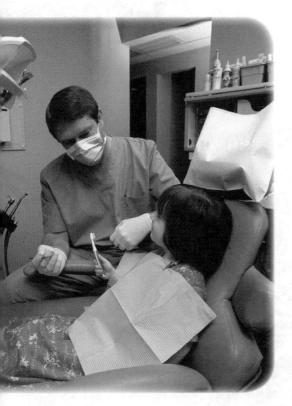

A **dentist** checks and
cleans your teeth.
He helps you have healthy
teeth.

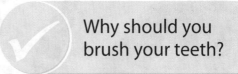
Why should you brush your teeth?

Safety

You should stay away from things that could hurt you. That is called being **safe**. Being safe is a way to take care of your body.

Be safe when you play. Wear a helmet when you ride a bike or a scooter. Obey the playground rules.

Put on your seatbelt in the car. A seatbelt helps keep you safe.

Be sure to stop, look, and listen before you cross a street.
Make sure an adult knows where you are.

God gave you your body.
You should take care of it.
Healthy, safe habits help you take care of your body.

What should you always put on when you are in the car?

Tame Animals

Pets

God created all the animals on the earth.
He made some big and some little.
He made some furry and some slippery.

God made some animals that
can live with people.
Tame animals live with people.
People take care of tame animals.

Pets are tame animals that
live in or around people's
homes.
Cats and dogs are pets.
Fish, rabbits, and birds
can also be pets.

You may have a pet you take care of.
What do you do to care for your pet?
You give your pet food and water.
You give your pet a place to stay.
You play with your pet.

Your pet might do things for you.
It might sing.
It might play with you.
It might help you.

What are tame animals?

Farm Animals

Some tame animals live on farms.
Cows, pigs, and sheep are **farm animals**.
Chickens, goats, and horses are also farm animals.

Farm animals need people to take care of them.
A farmer takes care of his farm animals.
He gives them the right food.
He gives them water.

A farmer gives his animals a safe place to live.
Some animals live in a barn.
Others may live in a pen or a coop.

What are some things a farmer gives to his animals?

Farm animals help people.
Cows and goats give milk.
Chickens lay eggs.
People get meat from some farm animals.

People also can get clothing from some farm animals.
Sheep have hair that is cut once a year.
This hair is called **wool**.
Wool can be used to make clothes.
It can be used to make blankets and coats.

Farm animals are used for work.
Horses can pull wagons and carts.
Some people ride horses to do work.
But people also ride horses just for fun.

The animals on a farm help the farmer.
They give him some things that he needs.
The farmer cares for the animals.
He gives them what they need.

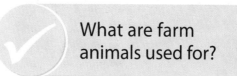

What are farm animals used for?

Zoo Animals

A zoo has many kinds of animals.
Some of the animals are tame.
You can touch them at the zoo.
But most zoo animals are not tame.
They are **wild animals**.

You might see tigers
and monkeys in a zoo.
Elephants and bears
may also live in a zoo.

At a zoo you get to see
animals from many
different places.
A zoo also helps
people study animals.

Some zoo animals stay in cages.
Other animals live in large outside places.
These places are much like where the animals
live in the wild.

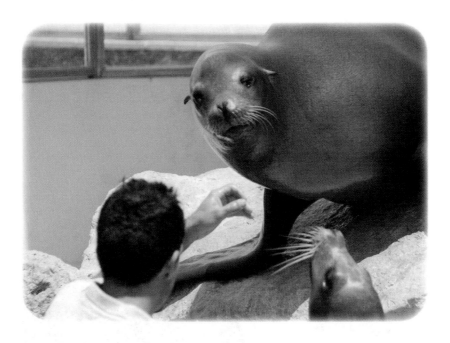

Zookeepers take care of the animals in a zoo.
They know what each animal needs.
They keep the animals' living spaces clean.
They give the animals food and water.
They take care of any animals that get sick.

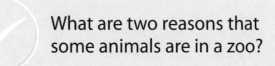

What are two reasons that
some animals are in a zoo?

Care of Animals

God gives animals what they need.
But He also wants people to care for animals.
In Proverbs the Bible tells people to take care
of animals.
A good man takes proper care of his animals.
We give glory to God when we take care of the
animals He made.

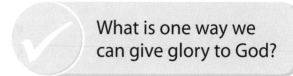
What is one way we
can give glory to God?

Process skill
● Classifying

Animal Homes

Every animal has a home. In this activity you will classify animals by where they live.

Purpose

Classify animals.

Materials
stuffed animals
Activity Manual

Procedure

1. Look at your stuffed animals. Think about where each animal would live.

2. Put each animal in the place where it would live.

3. Complete the *Animal Homes* page.

Conclusion

▶ Did any animals fit into more than one group?

Wild Animals

6

Wild Animals

Tame animals live with people.
But some animals do not live with people.
These animals are **wild animals**.

God takes care of wild animals.
He gives them what they need.

Wild animals make their own homes.
Beavers make a home in the water.
Birds make nests to lay their eggs in.
Spiders spin webs that catch food.

Every animal has a shelter, or home.
A **shelter** is a place where an animal can
be safe.

✓ What is a shelter?

73

Animal Tracks

Many times you do not see wild animals.
They may hide from people.
You might not be able to see an animal's home.
But you may see clues that show where the
animal has been.

A **print** shows the shape of an animal's foot.
Animals leave prints in snow, sand, or soft
ground.

A raccoon print looks like a child's hand.
Some bird prints show webbed feet.
The shape of a print helps us know which kind
of animal made it.

The size of a print also
tells us things about
the animal.
A mother bear makes
a larger print than her
bear cub does.

Tracks are prints that help us know what an
animal was doing or where it was going.

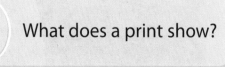

What does a print show?

Animal Marks

A **mark** is a clue that shows something about an animal.

Prints and tracks are kinds of marks.

But an animal leaves other marks too.

It may leave marks on trees and other plants.

A beaver chews on trees and cuts them down.

It uses the trees to build a home.

The beaver leaves a sharp point of wood.

The chewed tree is a mark.

This kind of mark shows that the beaver was there.

A woodpecker drills holes in trees.
It is looking for insects to eat.
You can see the marks where the woodpecker
looked for food.
This kind of mark tells you what the
woodpecker likes to eat.

God takes care of wild animals.
But you are more important to God than the
animals are.
He will take care of you.

What are some marks made by animals?

ACTIVITY

Animal Puppets

There are many wild animals. God made them all and cares for their needs. In this activity you will make an animal puppet and learn about that kind of animal.

Purpose

Make a model of an animal and learn what that animal needs.

Procedure

1. Use the paper bag and an animal pattern to make your puppet. Follow your teacher's directions.

2. Use craft materials to decorate your puppet.

Materials

paper lunch bag
Animal Patterns page
scissors
glue
craft materials
crayons or markers
Animal Notes page

3. Glue the animal note that fits your animal to the back of your puppet.

4. Show your puppet and tell others about your animal.

Conclusion

▶ In what ways does your puppet look like the real animal?

Matter

7

Matter

All the things around you are **matter**.
Your toys and games are matter.
Your food and drinks are too.
The air you breathe is matter.
Even your body is matter.
Your senses help you learn about the
matter around you.

Matter takes up space.
Matter can be weighed.
A rock is matter.
The rock takes up space.
It can be weighed.

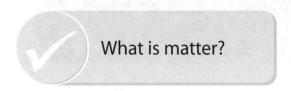

What is matter?

Solids

Matter comes in three forms.
It can be a solid, a liquid, or a gas.

Solid is a form of matter.
It can be weighed, and it takes up space.
A solid keeps its own shape and size.
When you move a solid, its shape and size
stay the same.

You may be able to color or bend a solid.
You may be able to change how it looks.
But a solid does not change
shape on its own.

A solid does not change size.
You may tear or cut a solid into pieces.
But all the pieces put together will be the same
size as the first piece.
The solid is still the same size.

 What happens to a solid
when you move it?

Liquids

Liquid is another form of matter.
A liquid is matter that flows.
It can be weighed and takes up space.

A liquid keeps its size.
But it does not keep its shape.
Its shape changes to fit its container.

Not all liquids are the same.
Some are thick.
A thick liquid flows slowly.
Honey is a thick liquid.

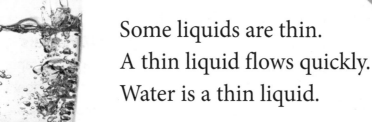

Some liquids are thin.
A thin liquid flows quickly.
Water is a thin liquid.

Some liquids mix together well.
Chocolate and milk mix together.
Other liquids, such as oil and
water, do not mix.
Water and oil stay apart from
each other.

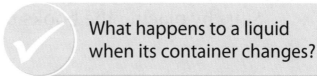

✓ What happens to a liquid
when its container changes?

ACTIVITY

Process skill
● Predicting

How Slow the Flow

Some liquids flow faster than others. It would take a long time to fill a glass of water if water flowed as slowly as honey. In this activity you will test liquids to see which flows slower.

Materials
masking tape
baking sheet
marker
3 books
prepared cups
Activity Manual

Problem

Which liquid flows slower?

Procedure

1. Use tape to mark a start line and a finish line for the liquid on the baking sheet. Label one line *Start* and the other *Finish*.

2. Record in your Activity Manual which liquid you think will finish last.

3. Raise the end of the baking sheet marked *Start* by placing the books under that end.

88

4. Have a friend help you tip the cups at the *Start* line so that the liquid flows out. Tip both the cups at the same time.

5. Observe the order in which the liquids finish. Record the order in your Activity Manual.

Conclusion

▶ Which liquid is thicker? How do you know?

Gases

Gas is another form of matter.
A gas can be weighed and takes up space.
But it does not keep its shape or its size.
It spreads out to fit the size and shape of its
container.

Gases are all around you.
Air is made up of different gases.
These gases mix together.
You breathe these gases all the time.

You cannot see gases.
But you can see what they do.

You use gases to blow up a balloon.

You blow a bubble with gum by filling the gum with gases.

Some gases can mix with liquids. The gases give the liquids a fizzy taste.

We use each form of matter in our lives every day.
Our wise God made all forms of matter for us to use and enjoy.

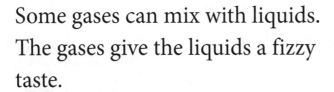

 What happens to a gas when its container changes?

Parts of Things

All objects are made of matter.
Most objects are made up of different parts.
The parts are made of matter too.

Different parts may have different jobs.
But all the parts are needed for the object
to work.

Some objects have only a few parts.
A kite has a few parts.
You can take the kite apart.
You can look at each of
the parts.
Then you can put the kite
back together.
The kite parts go together
to make a kite.

A car is an object with many parts.

It has a frame and wheels.

It has an engine.

The engine uses fuel.

Each of these parts is important for a car.

If any part is missing, the car will not run.

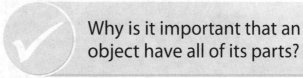

Why is it important that an object have all of its parts?

Sound

How Sound Is Made

You hear sounds all the time.
A friend laughs.
A bell rings.
A dog barks.
Hearing sounds helps you
observe God's world.

A sound is made when something moves
back and forth very quickly.
The moving is called a **vibration**.
Sound is a vibration that you can hear.

How do you make something vibrate?
You can hit it or rub it.
You can shake it or pluck it.
You can blow it.

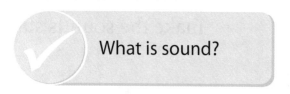

What is sound?

A Sound Band

Have you ever listened to a band play? All the band members make sounds by blowing, rubbing, shaking, hitting, or plucking. In this activity you will play a song by making sounds with instruments.

Purpose

Play a song using homemade instruments.

Materials
homemade
  instruments
Sound Band Song
pages

Procedure

1. Practice making sound using your instrument.

2. Get together with other students who have the same kind of instrument as you.

3. Practice making sounds as a group. Try to make the sounds start and stop together.

4. Look at the song you will play. Play the song several times together.

5. Listen as your teacher explains the letters that tell each group when to play.

6. Follow your teacher's directions and play the song.

Conclusion

▶ Which instrument was easiest to hear?

How Sound Moves

When you make a sound, you can hear it.
You cannot see sound moving.
But you can hear it moving.

Sound moves up and down.

Sound moves to the right
and to the left.

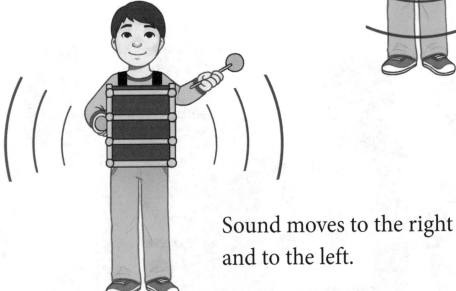

Sound moves in front of you and behind you.

Sound moves in all directions at the same time.

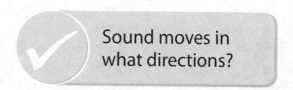

Sound moves in what directions?

Sound and Matter

Sound moves through all forms of matter.
Most of what we hear is sound that moves
through air.
Air is a gas.
Sound moves through gases.

Sound moves through liquids.
If you hit two rocks together
under the water, you can hear
the sound.
Sound moves through
the water.

Sound travels through solids.
You can hear some sounds outside of a room
even if the windows and doors are closed.
The walls, windows, and doors are solids.
Sound moves through these solids.

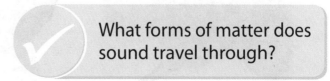

What forms of matter does
sound travel through?

Uses of Sounds

You hear sounds all day.
You listen to your friends as
they talk.
Maybe you hear birds singing.
You might hear cars on a road.

Some sounds are good for you to listen to.
Teachers help you learn about God's world.
Your parents tell you how to behave.
You should hear and obey what they say.
The Bible says that a wise person listens to
wise people.

Some sounds do not use words but still tell you something.
A fire alarm tells you to leave the building.
A siren tells drivers to move out of the way.
A hissing snake or a growling dog tells you to stay away.

God has given us the gift of sound.
He has given us ears to hear.
We should be thankful for these gifts He has given us.

 What is one sound that says something without words?

The Sun, Moon, and Stars

The Sun

God made the **sun**.
You can see the sun in the
sky during the daytime.
The sun is a star.
It is the star that is closest
to the earth.

The sun is very big.
It is bigger than the earth.

The sun is very hot.
It warms the earth.

The sun also gives light to the earth.
We need light to see.
Plants need light to make food.

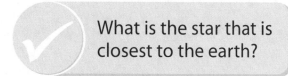
What is the star that is closest to the earth?

109

The Path of the Sun

The sun follows a path.
It moves across the sky
during the day.

At noon it is overhead.

In the evening the sun is in the west.
When the sun starts to disappear, it
is called **sunset**.

In the morning the sun is in the east.
When you first see the sun, it is called **sunrise**.

Where does the sun rise?

The Moon

God also made the **moon**.
The moon gives light at night.
The moon does not make its own light.
It **reflects** the light of the sun.

The moon is a big ball of rock.

The moon is closer to the earth than
the sun is.
It is smaller than the sun or the earth.

Some people have walked on the moon. These people are astronauts.
Astronauts are people who go into space.

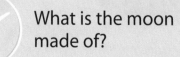
What is the moon made of?

The Moon's Shape

The moon seems to change shape.
We see only the part of the moon that is
reflecting the sun's light.
This part changes little by little each night.
We call these changes the phases of the moon.
It takes 28 days for us to see all the phases.

Sometimes we see just a small, thin sliver
of the moon.
It looks like a fingernail.
This is called a crescent moon.

crescent moon   quarter moon   full moon

Sometimes we see half the moon.
This is called a quarter moon.

Sometimes the moon looks like a big,
bright ball.
This is called a full moon.

Sometimes none of the moon is bright.
This is called a new moon.

✓ What is it called when we see only a sliver of the moon?

quarter moon   crescent moon   new moon

The Stars

God made many, many **stars**.
You see the stars in the sky at night.
They are far away from the earth.

You can see many stars just by looking at
the sky.
But to see even more stars you need a tool.
A **telescope** is a tool that helps you see
things that are far away.
With a telescope you can see more stars.

North Star —————•

Little Dipper

Big Dipper

Some groups of stars seem to make pictures.
One group of stars is called the Big Dipper.

One star is bright and easy to see.
It is called the North Star.
The North Star is part of a group of stars
called the Little Dipper.

✓ What tool can you use
to see more stars?

ACTIVITY

Stars in the Day

Stars shine all the time. We see the sun during the daytime. But we do not see many other stars in the daytime. In this activity you will find out why it is hard to see other stars during the day.

Materials
rubber band
aluminum foil
flashlight
pencil
white paper
Activity Manual

Problem

Why is it hard to see stars during the day?

Procedure

1. Use a rubber band to attach aluminum foil to the flashlight.

2. Use a pencil to poke a few small holes in the aluminum foil.

3. Shine the flashlight on a piece of white paper.

4. Record what you see in your Activity Manual.

5. Make the room dim. Shine the flashlight on the piece of paper.

6. Record what you see in your Activity Manual.

7. Darken the room. Shine the flashlight on the piece of paper.

8. Record what you see in your Activity Manual.

Conclusion

▶ Why is it hard to see stars other than the sun during the day?

Plants

Parts for Growing

God made many kinds of plants on the earth.
They are many sizes and shapes.
They are many different colors.

Plants may not all look the same.
But most plants have the same parts.
Most plants have roots, stems, and leaves.
Plants use these parts to grow.
Some plants also have flowers.

flowers

leaves

stems

roots

What are four parts of a plant?

Roots

Roots are the part of the plant that is under the ground.
The roots hold the plant in the ground.
The roots also take in water from the ground for the plant.

We eat some plants' roots.
Carrots and radishes are roots we eat.

Stems

A **stem** holds up the plant.
Water from the roots moves up the stem.
A tree trunk is a large stem.
The branches of a tree are also part of the stem.
The trunk and branches move water and food to all the parts of the tree.

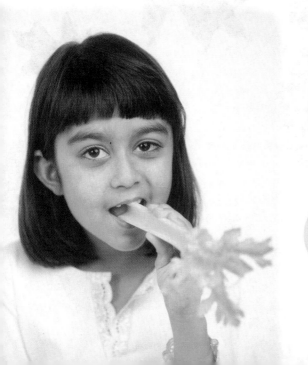

We eat some plants' stems.
Celery and asparagus are stems we eat.

 What part of a plant holds the plant up?

Leaves

Leaves make food for the plant.
They are many shapes and sizes.
The job of the leaves is to make food.

We eat some plants' leaves.
Lettuce and cabbage are leaves we eat.

Flowers

Many plants have flowers. **Flowers** make seeds for the plants.
The flowers also add color and beauty to the plants.

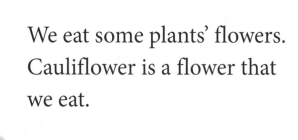

We eat some plants' flowers. Cauliflower is a flower that we eat.

✓ What do leaves do for a plant?

What Part?

Has your mother ever told you to eat your vegetables? Vegetables are plants that we can eat. In this activity you will decide which parts of the vegetable plants we eat.

Purpose

Decide what parts of plants we eat.

Materials
vegetables
grocery bags
Activity Manual

Procedure

1. Open the grocery bag you were given and take out the vegetables.

2. Look at each vegetable. Decide whether you would eat the root, the stem, the leaves, or the flowers.

3. Record in your Activity Manual which group you put each vegetable in.

4. Trade your bag with another science group. Record which groups the vegetables in the new bag belong in.

Conclusion

▶ Which group does your favorite vegetable belong in?

Flowers   Roots   Stems   Leaves

What We Make from Plants

We need plants for many reasons.
We get a lot of our food from plants.
But we also use plants for other things.
Plants are used to make some products.
A **product** is a thing people make from
something else.

Some foods you eat are products.
Grape jam is a product.
It is made from grapes.
Peanut butter is also
a product.
It is made
from peanuts.

Some products made from plants
are not foods.
Plants are used to make some
of your clothing.

Plants are used to make
paper products.

Plants are used to
make lumber.
Lumber is used for
houses and furniture.

God made plants for us to use and enjoy.

✓ What are two products that are made from plants?

What Plants Need

A plant needs four main things to grow.
It needs **air** and **light**.
The plant's leaves use air and light to
make food.

The plant also needs **water** and **soil**.
The water helps the plant get things
from the soil that it needs.

Soil is made of tiny rocks.
It also has small bits of dead plants and
animals in it.
These bits of dead plants and animals
help plants grow better.

Soil has living things in it too.
Some of these living things also
help plants grow.

God gave plants everything they need.
He takes care of them just as He takes
care of you.
Making plants for you to eat and use is
one way He takes care of you.

✓ What are four things that plants need to grow?

Forces

God made many things.
He made some things you can observe with your senses.
He made some things you cannot observe.
A **force** is a push or a pull.
You cannot observe a force.
But you can observe what a force causes things to do.

People, animals, and machines all use force.
We call this force **mechanical force**.
A person pushes or pulls a wagon.
A dog pulls on a leash.
A bulldozer pushes dirt.
Each time, a mechanical force is being used.

A force can start something moving.
When you throw a ball, you start the ball moving.

A force can also stop something moving.
When you catch a ball, you stop the ball from moving.

What is a force?

Friction

Sometimes it is hard to move an object.
Another force tries to keep it from moving.
That other force is friction.
Friction is a force that makes things slow
down or stop moving.
It happens when one thing rubs against
another thing.

Friction helps keep your feet from sliding.
It helps you walk and run without slipping.
It also helps you stop.

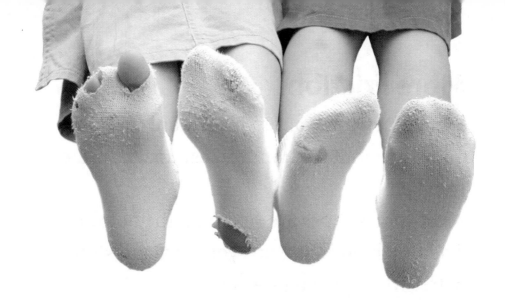

Friction causes things to wear out.
It can cause clothes to get holes in them.

Socks wear out from
rubbing against shoes
or the floor.
Sometimes the knees
in pants wear out.
The pants' knees rub
against many surfaces
as you play.

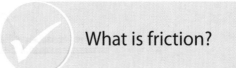

What is friction?

More Friction

Sometimes you want to have more friction.
To make more friction, you can make surfaces rougher.
Most sports shoes are rough on the bottom.
The rough bottom helps you start and stop better when playing sports.

Less Friction

Sometimes you want to have less friction.
One way to make less friction is to make surfaces smoother.
A smooth wood floor has less friction than carpet does.

Another way to have less friction is to have less surface to rub.
Ice skates have a small surface that rubs against the ice.
The skates have less friction than shoes do.

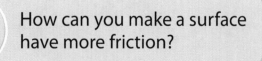
How can you make a surface have more friction?

Gravity

The earth also has a force.
The earth's force is called gravity.
Gravity is the force that pulls things toward the earth.
Gravity makes things come down.

You can throw a ball into the air.
Gravity pulls the ball back to the ground.
You can sit at the top of a slide.
Gravity tries to pull you down the slide.

Gravity causes someone who jumps from
a plane to fall to the ground.
A parachute catches air to help slow down
the person's fall.

Gravity is a force that keeps things on
the ground.
It keeps things from floating in the air.

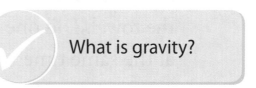

✓ What is gravity?

ACTIVITY

All Fall Down

Gravity pulls all things down. Suppose you drop a large object and a small object. Will one hit the ground first? Or will they hit at the same time? In this activity you will drop objects to see whether some things fall faster than others.

Problem

Do some objects fall faster than others?

Materials
thick towel
table tennis ball
softball
golf ball
piece of paper
Activity Manual

Procedure

1. Put the thick towel on the floor.
2. Have one student drop the table tennis ball and the softball from the height of a desktop.
3. Watch carefully to see when the balls hit the towel. Did one hit first? Or did they hit at the same time?

4. Record what happens in your Activity Manual.

5. Repeat the same procedure with the golf ball and the softball.

6. Crumple the piece of paper into a ball. Repeat again with the table tennis ball and the ball of paper.

Conclusion

▶ Did any object fall faster than another?

Magnetic Force

Magnets also have a force.
Magnets pull metal things that are
made of iron.
This force is called **magnetic force**.

You sometimes use magnets.
Maybe you play
some games that use
magnets.
Some magnets hold
things up.
Magnets may also be
used to hold things
together.

A magnet has two different ends, or **poles**.
One pole is called the north pole.
The other pole is the south pole.

The south pole of one magnet pulls the north pole of another magnet.
But the south pole pushes away the south pole of another magnet.

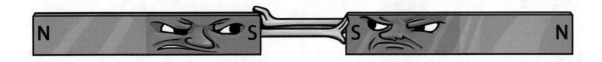

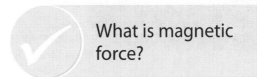

What is magnetic force?

God's World

God made a world with many things
for us to enjoy.
He gave us our senses so we can learn
about His world.
God gave us the job of using the
world He gave us.
We should be thankful for all the
things He has given us.
And we should be wise in our use of
what He has given us.
Doing so pleases Him.

 What does God want us to do with the world He made?

Glossary

A

astronaut   A person who goes into space.

autumn   A time of year when tree leaves change color and food is gathered.

C

clouds   Made of tiny drops of water in the air.

cycle   Something that happens over and over.

D

dentist   A person who checks and cleans teeth.

F

farm animals   Animals that live on a farm.

flowers   The part of a plant that makes seeds.

force   A push or a pull.

friction   A force that makes things slow down or stop moving.

G

gas   A form of matter that does not keep its shape or size.

germs   Things that can make a person sick.

gravity   The force that pulls things toward the earth.

H

habits   Things a person does over and over again.

healthy   Not sick or hurt.

hearing   Observing things with your ears.

L

leaves   The part of a plant that makes food for the plant.

liquid   A form of matter that keeps its size but takes the shape of its container.

M

magnetic force   The force that pulls things made of iron.

mark A clue that shows something about an animal.

matter Anything that has weight and takes up space.

mechanical force A force caused by people, animals, or machines.

moon A ball of rock in the night sky that reflects the sun's light.

O

observe To use your senses to find out something.

P

pets Tame animals that live in or around people's homes.

phases of the moon The different shapes of the moon.

poles The ends of a magnet.

print The shape of an animal's foot.

product   Something people make from something else.

R

record   To write down what you find out about something.

reflect   To bounce off.

report   To tell others about something.

roots   The part of a plant that is under the ground and holds the plant in place.

S

science   What you find out about the world.

scientist   A person who uses his senses to learn about God's world.

season   A time of year; spring, summer, autumn, or winter.

seeing   Observing things with your eyes.

senses   The ways God gave you to find out about the world; sight, touch, smell, taste, and hearing.

shelter   A safe place.

smelling   Observing things with your nose.

soil   Dirt.

solid   A form of matter that keeps its size and shape.

sound   A vibration you can hear.

spring   A time of year when baby animals are born and things are planted.

stars   Lights you can see in the night sky.

stems   The part of a plant that holds up the plant and moves water from the roots to parts of plant.

summer   A time of year when the daytime is long and things grow.

sun   The closest star to the earth. It gives heat and light to the earth.

sunrise   The time when the sun first shows in the east.

sunset   The time when the sun first starts to disappear in the west.

T

tasting   Observing things with your tongue and mouth.

teeth   Parts of your body used to cut and chew food.

telescope   A tool used to make things look larger.

temperature   How hot or cold something is.

thermometer   A tool used to find out the temperature.

touching   Observing things with your hands and fingers.

V

vibration   The moving of something back and forth very quickly.

W

weather   What the air outside is like.

weatherman   A person who tells about the weather.

wild animals   Animals that do not live with people.

wind   Moving air.

winter   A time of year when the daytime is short and plants and animals rest.

Z

zoo animals   Animals that live in a zoo.

zookeeper   A person who takes care of animals in a zoo.

Index

Photograph Credits

The following agencies and individuals have furnished materials to meet the photographic needs of this textbook. We wish to express our gratitude to them for their important contribution.

Air Force Special Operations Command (AFSOC)
Alamy, Inc.
BigStockPhoto.com
BJU Photo Services
Kim A. Cabrera
Channel 7 News
Corel
Eastman Chemicals Division
Fotolia
Getty Images
iStockphoto
JupiterImages Corporation
Susan Perry
PhotoDisc, Inc.
SuperStock
Thinkstock
Unusual Films
Visuals Unlimited, Inc.
Wikipedia

Chapter 1

© Ken Gillespie / Alamy vi–1; © Cristina Fumi / Alamy 4 (top); © Dana Rothstein. Image from BigStockPhoto.com 4 (bottom left); Getty Images/Comstock Images/Thinkstock 4 (bottom right), 6 (left); Getty Images/Creatas RF/Thinkstock 5; iStockphoto/Thinkstock 6 (right), 7 (top right), 8 (right), 9 (right), 11 (bottom), 14 (top left, top right), 15 (right); © xmasbaby/Fotolia 7 (top left); Getty Images/iStockphoto/Thinkstock 7 (bottom left); © Paul Maydikov. Image from BigStockPhoto .com 7 (bottom right); PhotoDisc, Inc. 8 (left), 9 (left); PhotoDisc/Getty Images 10 (top); Getty Images/Stockbyte/Thinkstock 10 (bottom); © Krzysztof Nieciecki. Image from BigStockPhoto.com 11 (top); BJU Photo Services 13: Getty Images/BananaStock RF/ Thinkstock 14 (bottom left); Unusual Films 14 (bottom right); © iStockphoto.com/akurtz 15 (left)

Chapter 2

© Exactostock / SuperStock 16–17; © iStockphoto.com/Olga Solovei 18 (left); © pelvidge/Fotolia 18 (center); iStockphoto/ Thinkstock 18 (right), 25; © iStockphoto .com/quidnunc 20 (left); Getty Images/ Comstock Images/Thinkstock 20 (right); Getty Images/iStockphoto/Thinkstock 22; PhotoDisc, Inc. 23; Digital Vision/Thinkstock 28 (top); Scientifica/Visuals Unlimited, Inc. 28 (bottom); Channel 7 News 29; BJU Photo Services 31

Chapter 3

Getty Images/Taxi 32–33; © Dennis Hallinan / Alamy 36; iStockphoto/Thinkstock 37 (top), 38, 39 (top), 42; Getty Images/iStockphoto/ Thinkstock 37 (bottom), 41 (top); Getty Images/Brand X/Thinkstock 39 (bottom); www.jupiterimages.com/Thinkstock 40; Hemera/Thinkstock 41 (bottom); Getty Images/MedioImages/Thinkstock 43; Getty Images/Photolibrary RM 43 (inset); BJU Photo Services 45

Chapter 4

Comstock/Thinkstock 46–47; Getty Images/ Thinkstock 48, 49 (left); iStockphoto/ Thinkstock 49 (right), 51 (bottom), 55 (top), 56 (bottom); © Ingrid Balabanova. Image from BigStockPhoto.com 51 (top); BJU Photo Services 53, 57; Getty Images/Digital Vision/ Thinkstock 54; Unusual Films 55 (bottom); Getty Images/Polka Dot RF/Thinkstock 56 (top)

Chapter 5

Photos.com/Thinkstock 58–59; © Eric Isselèe/Fotolia 60 (top); iStockphoto/ Thinkstock 60 (center), 66; Getty Images/ iStockphoto/Thinkstock 60 (bottom), 63 (top); Getty Images/Dorling Kindersley 61 (left), 63 (bottom); Don Farrall/PhotoDisc/

Getty Images 61 (right); © Baerbel Schmidt/
Getty Images 62; Corel 63 (center); © Juniors
Bildarchiv / Alamy 64 (top); © Juice Images/
Fotolia 64 (bottom); Lifesize/Getty Images/
Thinkstock 65; © MarkaBond/Fotolia 67;
© WILDLIFE GmbH / Alamy 68; BJU Photo
Services 69

Chapter 6

PhotoDisc, Inc. 70–71, 73 (bottom left), 77;
iStockphoto/Thinkstock 72; © iStockphoto
.com/HarryKolenbrander 73 (top); Hemera/
Thinkstock 73 (bottom right); Kim A.
Cabrera/www.beartracker.com 75 (top
left); Dave King/Dorling Kindersley/Getty
Images 75 (top right); Getty Images/National
Geographic 75 (bottom); PhotoDisc/Getty
Images 76; BJU Photo Services 79

Chapter 7

© Exactostock / SuperStock 80–81; BJU Photo
Services 83 (both), 84 (both), 85 (all), 86
(both), 89, 90 (both); iStockphoto/Thinkstock
83 (rock); © iStockphoto.com/LiseGagne 87
(left); © iStockphoto.com/OlgaMiltsova 87
(right); © iStockphoto.com/Kathleen Melis 91
(top left); Getty Images/Hemera/Thinkstock
91 (top right), 92; Getty Images/iStockphoto/
Thinkstock 91 (bottom)

Chapter 8

AbleStock.com/Thinkstock 94–95; Getty
Images/Hemera/Thinkstock 96 (top);
© iStockphoto.com/Vikram Raghuvanshi 96
(center); Hemera/Thinkstock 96 (bottom);
BJU Photo Services 99, 103; PhotoDisc, Inc.
102 (top); © iStockphoto.com/Michael Ivanin
102 (center); © Paul Springett 01 / Alamy 102
(bottom); iStockphoto/Thinkstock 104 (top);
© Rob/Fotolia 104 (bottom); © AshDesign/
Fotolia 105 (left); © Art_man/Fotolia 105
(right)

Chapter 9

© Exactostock / SuperStock 106–7; Getty
Images/iStockphoto/Thinkstock 108; Getty
Images/Hemera/Thinkstock 109; iStockphoto/
Thinkstock 112; Eastman Chemicals Division
113; Luc Viatour/Wikipedia/GNU Free
Documentation License/Creative Commons
Attribution-Share Alike 3.0 Unported 114–15
(all); BJU Photo Services 119

Chapter 10

© Photononstop / SuperStock 120–21;
iStockphoto/Thinkstock 122, 126 (top right,
bottom), 131 (top); BJU Photo Services 123,
129, 131 (center); © Cultura / Alamy 124;
Getty Images/Dorling Kindersley 125 (left);
Hemera/Thinkstock 125 (right); © Noam/
Fotolia 126 (left); Getty Images/Hemera/
Thinkstock 126 (top center right), 127 (top);
PhotoDisc, Inc. 126 (bottom center right);
© iStockphoto.com/IgorDutina 127 (bottom);
© D. Hurst / Alamy 130; © 2009 JupiterImages
Corporation 131 (bottom)

Chapter 11

AFSOC/Senior Airman Jason Epley 134–35;
© Arco Images GmbH / Alamy 136 (top);
Getty Images/Hemera/Thinkstock 136
(bottom); Getty Images/Stone 137; Susan
Perry 139 (top); Getty Images/iStockphoto/
Thinkstock 139 (bottom), 148 (right); Brand
X Pictures/Thinkstock 142; © Stockbroker /
MediaMagnet / SuperStock 143; BJU Photo
Services 145; © Fancy / Alamy 146; Creatas/
Thinkstock 148 (left); © clearviewstock.
Image from BigStockPhoto.com 149 (top
left); © Choups / Alamy 149 (top right);
iStockphoto/Thinkstock 149 (bottom left);
Getty Images/Digital Vision/Thinkstock 149
(bottom right)